COURAGE

Find Your Fire and Ignite Action in Your Life

GLENDA BENEVIDES

ISBN: 978-0-578-84120-5

Library of Congress Control Number: 2021900958

Editing, design, and layout by Backspace Ink

This book is dedicated to three exceptional, brave, and courageous human beings who have deeply and unmistakably touched my life in so many ways. These three men underlined the power of being direct, speaking the truth, and supporting me to fully be who I am. I could write volumes on their qualities and extraordinary lives: from working for the government and then from jail, from bull riding to the jungles of South America, from abuse to forgiveness, and for ultimately standing for love.

Sunil Bhaskaran demonstrated the power of perseverance while standing for compassion, understanding, grace, and most of all the heart of love in someone else's world.

Gene Williams modeled consistent excitement for life's adventures, matched with a fervor and an ongoing daily practice of sharing his gratitude. He truly saw me as a magnificent artist, helping me to shine brightly.

Robert Mitchell pointed out that, no matter how bad or badass your life is, you can always shift anything and bring it up a notch in the right mindset.

I love you all so much. I am a better woman for knowing you, walking a path with you, and knowing that you trust me while sharing your life.

Contents

Preface

My intention and desire in writing this book is that you will begin to see how important you are in your own world and in the world of others in your life. You will need a separate, personal journal to write down answers to some questions that I'll pose as well as your thoughts, inspirations, and insights.

It all starts with a sincere foundation of love and care for yourself. The foundation is YOU. With a solid foundation, you will create building blocks to confidence and experience courage to get what you want with grace and flow.

With a foundation of self-love and self-care, you will create a space to experience freedom in your life and for the people around you. This freedom comes from taking the time to develop powerful habits and mindful ways of being, which will set you on an extraordinary path to your own empowerment.

When you follow your clear path, you will develop new skills, new attitudes, an inspired vision of who you are and who you are not, and the passion to step into your true heart's desire. You will have courage—and all that comes with it—in every choice you make. As you move forward to create breakthroughs and see new possibilities, you are on a path to self-discovery.

Extraordinary people say "yes" and then act. Reading this book is the first step—and you've taken it!

Glossary

badass: Someone who is clear, self-possessed, straightforward, and courageous

badass goddess: A woman who is confident, compassionate, and never needs justification for who she is and is not; she activates courage to express herself and uses her unique qualities to empower others around her

global badass goddess: A conscious, courageous, self-expressed, and empowered woman

goddess: also known as the sacred female or the sacred feminine, a woman to be admired for who she is and for her virtues

high priestess: A divine woman who has prowess of her body, mind, and spirit

magician: A person with exceptional skills in a particular area and who discovers hidden knowledge

number "11": Double numbers are considered master numbers. In numerology, these numbers are considered to be connections to a higher source of wisdom. The duty of number "11" is to use the gift of awareness to deliver cosmic truths that encourage humanity. This number carries harmony, empathy, and sensitivity. Being a "1" as well, it's innovative and motivated and open to new things to make a difference. It makes a creative leader, an active listener, and a compassionate advisor. This master number's vision is crystal clear and sees with a breadth that others cannot. It's creative and magnetic, a beacon of wisdom, and an inspiration for others to follow.

INTRODUCTION

COURAGE

Foundation of Self-Love

Courage—we all have it, but sometimes accessing it can be illusive.

You can find the access point to courage with a foundation of self-acceptance and self-love. This foundation allows your gifts, talents, and honest desires to be present, moving you forward into your light and allowing you to share yourself more fully and freely.

Do you want to:

- ♥ Play a bigger game?
- ♥ Take your courage and confidence to a new level?
- ♥ Reveal what's possible and what's hidden?
- ♥ Move yourself into a more fulfilling life purpose?
- ♥ Get more out of life?
- ♥ Be fully expressed?
- ♥ Love deeply?
- ♥ Be free?
- ♥ Step into your alignment with distinction and truth?

COURAGE

♥ Be the courageous, unthinkable gift that you are?

If your answer is "yes" to any or all of the above questions, this book is for you.

Running from one task to another—with no idea of who you are, what you are, and what you want from moment to moment—erodes your inner light and steals your energy. Then, one day you realize that there's nothing left.

You may not have confidence, but you can have courage to reach out, inquire, open up, and grow. Facing something new and uncomfortable takes audacity and bravery. Getting out of bed for some people *is* courage. Saying "I am going to start again today and work on my passions" *is* courage. By activating courage, you are one step closer to doing the unthinkable.

There is a way out of feeling stuck, disenchanted, and alone. You don't have to be relegated to the lies you tell yourself— especially the biggest lie: "I cannot have what I truly desire."

What you have to offer, share, or give to others is worthy enough to be explored, designed, dreamed, created, or produced for all to experience. Telling your stories may save someone else's life or hearing someone else's music may move you through a painful emotion. When you hear words of wisdom, they may shift and uplift your life.

It's time to do the unthinkable.

Step forward—*empowered*—on the path of your dreams.

COURAGE IS THE FIRE THAT IGNITES YOUR TRUTH

Freedom is a way of being, and your every breath is an act of rebellion.

—Glenda Benevides

Embracing the Truth

You are capable of having courage, but you need to commit to it. Getting excited and saying you're committing to something is the easy part; however, all the complexities underneath can trip you up.

You "flow and go" in some areas of your life (e.g., getting up and making a call, designing a company, and making a move). Then, you may spend much of your time avoiding other things (e.g., "I'll get to that later"). It's simple yet complicated. Ultimately, such behavior is painful and can leave you frustrated and unfulfilled.

The First Stage of Courage: Willingness

Courage has stages, just like most things in life, and the first stage is willingness. Courage requires a willingness to dig into what and who you are because who you are now starts the journey. When you come face to face with your honest desires, you can take inventory of what you are truly passionate about and what you've been ignoring or hiding.

Once you understand that your passion is not going away, you will be able to creatively solve the problem of doing it. This understanding will put you on the same page with yourself and with no one else—no judgment, no comparison.

Finding and sorting out your passion and desire may take a little time, but you will be curious about the question of "how." Listen, wait for the answers, and *be patient*. The answers will show up, piece by piece.

The Second Stage of Courage: Commitment

The next stage of courage is about trying things on, and that takes commitment.

Commitment often feels like it's coming from outside of yourself—like someone else is deciding your future and telling you what to do. You may feel rebellion toward it, the urge to avoid it, or even the desire to start an insurrection. You may feel like a child with a temper tantrum or have a teen's rebellious attitude.

These reactionary games may feel victorious, but you ultimately become the loser. Temper-tantrum mindsets can become repetitive, ingrained patterns with little or no positive results, controlling your choices and leaving you with no freedom or options for empowerment.

Contrary to these false beliefs, you can take back your power by owning your life through your intentional mindset and a practice of conscious choice. Courage patterns follow naturally.

♥ You are not a victim.

♥ You are a powerful being.

♥ You can achieve full self-expression.

Whom are you fighting against? No one but you! No one is making you do *anything*.

Your mind has made up an illusion, a repetitive pattern to believe in and follow, repeating it over and over like an unconscious knee-jerk reaction.

It's time to stop the repetitive madness!

There's good news. *You can retrain.*

The Third Stage of Courage: Retraining

The final stage of courage is about retraining. Your mind is malleable, and you can retrain and repattern your old thoughts into new thoughts and realign your beliefs. This process supports others in knowing who you are today, now. You can choose the design of your life in alignment with your current true desires.

Truly knowing the value of who you are and what you have to share can be difficult at times. It is the foundational fire that supports and fuels every experience in life—the driving core belief that you are good enough, worthy enough, brave enough, and smart enough to be, do, and have whatever you say it is. It is the knowledge that you belong and that this shining value or lack of value gives you the color of the sky you walk under and the kind of flow in the river you swim in.

It is best to create a value and a belief that says, "I am valuable. Here I am, and I am who I am."

Actively valuing and designing a belief that supports confidence and empowerment allows for clear communication and commitment to your naked truth. Knowing your true value keeps life present and active in choices that serve your highest good and delightfully serves others in return.

Awareness, Choice, Commitment, and Freedom

Choose the steps to start the journey toward what you are passionate about and willing to commit to, and then put your energy behind them. You will be ready for clear commitment to yourself. This clarity with passion allows action and movement to flow in all directions with ease. This awareness—making a choice and staying with the commitment—keeps a wonderful structure in place for you to have a roadmap, which makes action and movement a little easier.

Without all these things, you will only have a dream of a someday, one-day life—never to be seen, felt, or marvelously experienced.

Look in the mirror and embrace all that you are. It's time to pursue you and the steps that bring you and your hidden dreams into alignment.

Allow your life to be joyful, fulfilled, successful, and free!

THE 4 AS: ALIGNMENT, ACCOUNTABILITY, AMPLIFICATION, AND ACTION

Speaking your truth and using your voice
is a commitment to what you believe.

—Glenda Benevides

THE 4 AS: ALIGNMENT, ACCOUNTABILITY, AMPLIFICATION, AND ACTION

The First A: Alignment

....
a·lign·ment
/əlīnmənt/
a position of agreement or alliance
....

B egin with an honest understanding of who you are now. This is always the first step in allowing yourself to have a clearly integrated and empowered direction.

It starts by asking yourself these types of questions:

♥ "Who am I and what am I aligned with?"

♥ "What do I want?"

♥ "What don't I want?"

♥ "Will I stick to my choices no matter how someone pulls on my heart strings or tries to manipulate me?"

This awareness is paramount in creating alignment; otherwise, people or situations will drain you dry and leave you with nothing but complaints and confusion.

Create a declaration of independence—a kind of mission statement for yourself or an alignment list. Make it something you can live by and refer to when the sea gets rough or when you catch yourself going back to old habits. Take the time to know yourself today, right now, and design yourself without constraints.

Alignment is an ongoing thing. It happens daily, weekly, and yearly. What you love, desire, and care about will change, yet your core declaration and ways of being will stay clear and begin to get stronger. If you don't take the time to create what is key for you, it's easy to be buried by fears and confusion.

Once you have a core structural foundation of who you are, you will find that situations will either go away or you will clear things up and reset boundaries that fit into your life's declaration and are in alignment with your life.

The act of writing things down reinforces what you already have, what you want, and what you don't want in your life. In your journal, create your alignment list.

For example, you may write:

- ♥ "I have people in my life who love and support me in ways that serve the greater experience between us."
- ♥ "I continue to remind myself that how I listen to others is from a place of love and compassion."
- ♥ "When people are angry, I know that it is not necessarily at me. I ask questions in curiosity to clarify."

♥ "I am aligned with my inner patience and guidance and interact from there."

♥ "I refuse to do business with people who are only focused on themselves."

When you align with your higher ideals, life flows in an upward direction.

The Second A: Accountability

ac·count·abil·i·ty
\ ə-ˌkaȯn-tə-ˈbi-lə-tē \
an obligation or willingness to accept
responsibility or to account for one's actions

Accountability plays a huge part in all of life. If you are accountable for you, being responsible for what you do or say in life is the key to flow and ease. Although it sometimes takes just a minute, it can be the hardest to do.

Blaming things and others may be your first reaction, but it's only a clever illusion of fear. In any conflict or upset, you may want to resist and make things wrong instead of just being quiet and curious and seeing your part in the equation.

If you can accept what is, shift your mindset, and stop positioning, you can pull down the wall of illusion and fear to see your part. This wall will keep you from your self-expression and freedom. Once the wall is down, you'll quickly move toward peace without guilt or making yourself wrong. When you step into your accountability, inner balance begins to shine.

If you are blaming others or not seeing your part, you are taking yourself out of being responsible. You lose your access to harmony, alignment, balance, strength, and ultimate freedom.

It is easy to not see that the source is YOU. Wherever you go, there you are. It is up to you to see where you fit into the equation in every situation. Once you take a minute to do this, your power is restored.

It's a crazy equation. Your attitude to match whatever shows up is key. Seemingly out of the blue and sometimes unannounced, *insane* happens—where the rubber meets the road. This is when your core being is called into action. How do you respond, and do you rise above it?

When you start to see your part in each scenario and be willing to be accountable—especially when people are upset— you can choose to respond appropriately to them. Keep calm and keep trying.

What's appropriate? When you leave a situation, you feel complete, and the situation is in forward motion with a sense of freedom actively restored. You are complete, and you've done your best.

Accountability is the way we stay empowered and account for what we say, do, and create. There's no right or wrong—only what we've created.

The Third A: Amplification

....

am·pli·fi·ca·tion
/ˌamplifiˈkāSH(ə)n/
the action of making something larger or greater (as in amount, importance, or intensity) to increase its strength
....

Amplifying and committing to something is to do it daily with passion, perseverance, and expansion that you won't give up on.

When you can see clearly what you want to do, it's much easier to stay on the road to your dreams, visions, and passions in life. Time seems to be suspended and doors seem to open a little easier and faster when you have a clear path and a solid commitment. You tend to wake up every morning with excitement and love in your heart, ready for the next adventure and challenge.

Commitment is not easy when faced with daily challenges, especially when they are emotional, mental, or even physical.

The goal or the mission becomes a labor of love and fulfillment. There will always be a belief around a perceived challenge, and you'll have to rise above that inner monologue.

This monologue will tell you many negative stories of why you cannot do or be something. You'll have to face it and learn to work with it until that nagging voice gets smaller and eventually, with practice, will go away. Once you embrace who you are, you will gain a muscle in your commitment mindset and be honest about what you *really* want to do. Then the commitment comes a bit more easily.

Letting go of others' ideals, dreams, and opinions of what and who "you" should be can be a difficult hurdle. It is often uncomfortable to deal with others' disapproval. Hang on. Once you can be with this discomfort, you will find yourself in a place of naturally wanting to set time aside to think about what you want or what new skills you'll need to incorporate on your path. This new way of being will add to your newfound commitment to amplify YOU.

The truth about commitment is that it aligns a framework for partnership and accountability within yourself. This allows creativity and freedom to grow and flow.

The Fourth A: Action

....

ac·tion

/ˈakSH(ə)n/

the fact or process of doing something,

typically to achieve an aim

....

Ask yourself these questions:

♥ "What am I doing to cause an outcome in my physical dimension/world?"

♥ "Am I causing an action around my inner plane/world?"

♥ "What am I thinking about?"

♥ "What am I feeling?"

♥ "What actions or nonactions are causing me to move (or not move) in my life?"

The mind is a terrible thing when unchecked. Mental gymnastics of nonsense can lead you down a destructive path of lies. You are then frozen to the actions that need to be taken for the forward movement of your dreams. Freedom is not present if you say "no."

It's complicated, but it's possible. It takes truly knowing yourself and being straight about your bad habits and fears. Understand the lies that you are telling yourself to stop you from anything that means freedom. Being accountable takes clarity about everything. Then add commitment, which can create a structure of freedom to release your passions.

Motivate your movement and actions with purpose. If you have these steps in place, you will most likely create an action plan. You may need to set up a call with a close friend who will support you in what you are committed to and help you on a weekly basis in order to get things accomplished.

Action expresses your priorities, and actions speak louder than words.

Reach Out and Jump In

Partnerships are fun, create deep connections, help with sticky spots, and are very empowering when you actually have to reach out to someone and ask. Some of you may have to get over that hurdle to simply reach out.

If, that happens, go back to asking yourself, "What am I committed to?"

Once you remember and feel the flow, you will get on the phone and ask! There is a huge breakthrough waiting for you if you are willing to jump in.

CHAPTER 3

EMBRACE WHO YOU ARE, ASK FOR WHAT YOU WANT, AND SPEAK UP

If you are alive and breathing, you are growing no matter what you believe or what is happening.

—Glenda Benevides

You Are Who You Say You Are

Get present and take a moment to ask yourself, "Who am I?" Ask yourself this ever-evolving, truth-seeking question every day and ponder it with curiosity. Embracing yourself *as you are* is a key factor in being able to move anything forward in this world as an honest, empowered manifestation of the authentic YOU.

Embrace all the parts of yourself *as they are* and then take inventory. Identify the components of your social design and decide what is truly you, what has been picked up from outside sources, and if your core beliefs have been long outgrown.

These core beliefs are stories that run your life, whether or not you like them. Make a concerted, conscious effort to redesign any ideals and patterns that hold you back and lie to you about who you are, such as telling yourself that you couldn't or shouldn't do something.

Take the time to step back and reevaluate your life. This action will support your efforts to embrace your own thoughts, inspirations, and honest desires and sort out the inner monologue that is working against you. Look at your own truth and intentionally let go of others' opinions. The walls of fear take the wind out of the sails of courage. Own what are truly your feelings. Speak up and speak out with passion and fervor, and love who you are.

It is time to stand for YOU, to share, to be aware, and to be conscious that you are someone who wants more. This beginning stage will shift your lifestyle, your path, and your dream. Most of all, it will shift your state of being. Start your day knowing and standing in who you are.

Ask Yourself Who You Are and What You Want

Take time to ask yourself—uninterrupted—and truly ponder this question: "Who am I now?"

Your answer may be, "I am a woman who cares deeply for the well-being of our planet and who loves to sing, write, and raise the consciousness of all people."

Once you have your answer, write it down in your journal. Write from a place of naked honesty. *This journal is for you and no one else.* Be with who you are and what you might want, and see how that feels.

If it feels good, write more about it with no judgment. Keep going.

Sitting with what you want—with no pressure—and being clear and honest, asking questions, and receiving answers will be exciting and frightening. Ask yourself deep questions and be transparent.

Ask yourself, "What do I want now?"

Your answer should come from a desire to achieve fulfillment and service in your life, such as places you've never visited, people whom you've wanted to meet, and things you always wanted to do but never did.

Choose a Fulfilling Life

Take a second, stop, close your eyes, take a deep breath, and ask yourself, "Am I truly fulfilled in my life?"

You may be scared to write down the answer, so don't rush. Just feel it in your body, and then feel it in your emotional self, your inner self, your spiritual self, your higher self, your soul self … whatever self you want to call it.

Calmly ask this question again: "Am I truly fulfilled?"

Think about what you truly and passionately want and write the answer in your journal.

For example, you may write, "I've always wanted to run my own business and sell the jewelry I make" or "I've always wanted to live in Italy and have a winery."

If your answer to the fulfillment question is "yes," then rock on.

If your answer to the fulfillment question is anything other than "yes," take a minute, ask yourself why you are not fulfilled, and write the answers in your journal.

Your answers may be:

♥ "I am not fulfilled because I don't love myself, and other people's opinions are more important than mine."

♥ "I am afraid to go to Italy because my family may not support me or want to go."

♥ "Someone told me that making jewelry is silly and not a sustainable way to make a living."

In your journal, write what would truly fulfill you. Reflect and understand what might be missing or stopping you in your life. Keep looking and be curious with yourself—*for yourself.* There is no right or wrong answer.

You may write, "I would be fulfilled by taking time off work to plan what I really want, getting private and personal coaching to find out how to transition my life to Italy, finding a job, playing guitar every day, and getting a local gig in one month." Maybe it's a career choice that you never made, somewhere you wanted to move, someone you wanted to marry but didn't, or a guitar you wanted to play.

Perhaps your parents said, "You're going to college, so don't think about joining that band" or "We're not paying for college or wasting our time and money on you." *Blah blah blah!*

Others' negative opinions soon become yours along with a "what if?" fear factor. No matter how much they love, care, or think about you, they do not know what's best for you. Walk your own path without fear, jump out, try new things, find yourself, and live your dreams and ideals. It's about YOU.

If you are not truly living with purpose, joy, passion, excitement, love, and freedom, it's time to choose something truly right for you. When you take the step toward your choices, you will find that *the juice of life is the juice of you.*

Things that keep you from having an expanded and fulfilled life can be hidden in helpful words or not so hidden in the barrier of outright lies of someone else's agenda. Be honest with yourself, own it, let it be, and then choose a new commitment to start again.

When you uncover self-deception, momentum begins. You will need courage to step out of self-deception, to write your feelings down, and to say things aloud to yourself. The real challenge is to unravel years of false stories, fears, and other people's truths about you. It can be done, piece by piece.

Choose to step forward, be brave, and commit to breaking free. It's a simple and challenging step, but it's a journey worth taking. Take a moment and remember one thing that would fulfill a deep, unfilled desire. Once you identify this desire, you can begin to chart a course, organize it, and ultimately realize it.

As you grow and move through life, you are always evolving. Remember all the things you did and said when you were in high school that you don't do or say anymore. You evolved, shifted, changed, and made new choices.

Now, at this moment, it is time to stand up for YOU.

My Early Life Lessons

I had an opportunity to "find myself" relatively unobstructed by my parents' desires and ideals while growing up. As an only child, I mostly took care of myself and made choices based on what I felt was honest, true, and from the heart. My parents taught me basic principles of respect, care for all things, and kindness. The rest of my inner design was up to me. I had the freedom to sort out the rest of life on my own.

My parents taught me to share my things, take care of other people's belongings as if they were my own, and replace things if they were broken. They also said to respect people and their property and to ask for things and not just take something. Most of all, they taught me to be mindful of others, not to be rude, and to stand up for myself. This was my foundation.

These qualities gave me a clear view to see life and myself in a way that supported who I was becoming. As I grew and developed, I spoke up and cared. I was thoughtful, mindful, and kindhearted. I nurtured and inspired others.

I care about people, animals, and loving connections, among other things. I continue these qualities as a lifelong way of being.

Second-Grade Abuse and Bullying

You truly learn who you are when your foundational beliefs are tested. This first test hit me early in life when we moved from East Oakland, California, to Salem, Oregon. Salem was small town at the time (about 60,000 people), which was a real shock. I felt like a lost, fearful outsider.

In the second grade, I was faced with the "who am I?" moment at the age of seven. Our first-period English teacher was an intolerant woman who would often pull my hair if I raised my hand and asked too many questions. She would also take one particular student out of the class and go into another room. Everyone would jump up and run into the coat closet as if we were going to recess. It was weird, but I would follow them.

One day, I heard a horrible and muffled noise, a whack, and then a cry. The little autistic girl in our class was being beaten! I remember how sudden, brash, and odd it was. I thought that having a teacher beat a child at school was strange, shocking, upsetting, and wrong. My seven-year-old mind thought that the little girl had done nothing to deserve this treatment. I felt that the teacher should have shown patience and refrained from daily beatings of a little girl who was intellectually disabled.

Even though I was new in town and felt fear, I still had to do something. I had had enough of the bullying and my own abuse. When I got home that night, I told my dad what was happening even though I was afraid of how he might react. I knew it was the right thing to do. I needed to stand up for myself and the autistic student and try to stop the bullying and the madness. I was scared to tell my parents, but it was more horrifying for that little girl on a daily basis. My father—a military man—would have none of it.

Honesty and Truth Go Beyond Fear

From this experience, I learned that even if there is pain and humiliation in a situation, it doesn't necessarily make you want to speak your truth or even stand up for what is right. It takes courage to face your own fear of being ridiculed or ousted.

Somehow for me, though, I didn't care. I knew that it wasn't right and that someone had to speak up. I was not going to let fear stop me from helping another person and being true to myself.

I won't tell you what my father said to that teacher or to the principal the next day, but I will tell you that it stopped. After speaking the honest truth, I knew that I could stand up and speak up to right the things that were wrong. It always pays to do something that moves you or seems like an injustice.

Speak your mind and your heart, and feel the freedom of doing so.

DESIGN AND CREATE YOUR OWN INTENTIONS

Dream and give yourself permission to envision a You that you can choose to be.

—Joy Page

My Foundation of
Love and Support

My life's story and passion are about singing. I've met so many people along my journey who have said that they always wanted to sing or that they did sing a bit in the high school choir, but they never continued it as a profession, and they're not sure why.

As I embraced who I was early in my life, I knew that I wanted to keep singing and do it for a living. It was a natural gift for me. My parents were always supportive and came to almost every play and choir performance. When I join my first band, they would drive to other states to hear me sing and perform.

I felt very fortunate and grateful to have had the experience of being able to do what I loved without any negative words, attitudes, or attempts to persuade me to take other paths. Of course, there were other struggles along the way, but my parents' support of my dream and their love, honor, and acceptance of me was never an issue. I was always allowed to develop what I was, in my own way. This early support gave me the padding to tackle my inner fears, to keep going, to not give up, and to be brave.

As I developed my own sense of artistic ability, doors opened and I naturally moved toward them. Then, daily practice, patience, and real commitment were required. When challenges came, they kept me straight about my true desires and passion and let me know right away if my intentions and desires were in alignment.

Set Up Your Support Foundation

Of course, you may not have a supportive family or friends and may struggle with all types of hurdles. However, you and what you want are none of their business. It's yours and yours alone.

If you have had no support or agreement in your life, you will need to set up this foundation for yourself and then build and develop this muscle. If what you are doing is not freeing, move to the next passion. Inside and the other side of the challenge are gifts of freedom and service.

You have what you need to evolve the way you need to evolve. Your experience is unique to you, so dive in. The hard challenges of your journey don't mean that you have to give up or let go of having your desires and dreams. It's just a little trickier at times.

The key is to keep going. You may have to overcome something while doing some heavy lifting in the emotional or belief systems department of your mind, but it can be done … step by step.

Time to Move Forward

Now that you have explored who you are and have committed to embrace YOU fully, you are ready to design and create your own intentions.

Choose one thing that you've decided to move forward on. For example, maybe you've always wanted to sing or play an instrument, move across the country, quit your job, or reach out and share what you truly want with a friend.

Start to create opportunities for yourself. In your journal, at the top of the page, write "My Dream." Be brave and just do it! Then, underneath your dream word or sentence, add "My Intention." You can do this for everything you want. Don't worry about how you're going to get it or get there. It will come. This step in writing it down is huge and will free some of your hidden desires.

Here are a couple of examples:

♥ Under the "My Dream" heading, you can write, "My dream is to be a professional singer and songwriter."

♥ Under the "My Intention" heading, you can write, "My intention in singing is to fully express my passion and love for music by using my voice and writing lyrics with music that deeply inspire, excite, and move people. Through my heartfelt storytelling, I want to bring awareness to current challenges in our communities that inspires solutions. I want to do this at least twice a week and be compensated for it."

Answer the following questions and write your answers in your journal:

♥ "What is my unfulfilled desire and intention?"

♥ "What is my purpose?"

♥ "What are the set beliefs that aren't supporting me now?"

♥ "What am I willing to give up or let go?"

♥ "What is my next step on the road to fulfillment?"

A Deeper Look

These questions and exercises will give you a deeper look at what is hidden or what you have been circling, ignoring, and resisting. When you do this work with wonder and a joyful mindset, you will learn new and insightful things about yourself and have a sense of curiosity and play in the things that you've always wanted to do.

Make it fun! This could be a new journey of discovery and possibilities.

CHAPTER 5

TAKE THE FIRST STEP TOWARD YOUR DREAMS OF DESIRE AND FIRE

Sometimes the gift comes
when you least expect it.

—Glenda Benevides

Adjust the Plan As You Go

In Chapter 4, I shared a story about my choice to be a professional singer. I also described how the doors opened more easily because I initially developed a clear intention and took steps out of love and passion with sheer ignorance. On some level, I knew that I could do whatever I set my mind to, even if I were afraid and had no idea as to what I should do or be prepared for.

That "jumping in" moment eventually revealed the many levels I had to go through to make singing a real career. For you, the moment is now, and the key is to *just start*. Come up with a plan, stay with it, go forward, and adjust it as you go. You will get there.

Ignorance is bliss. It's time to move into that feeling, like being 16 years old again. It's truly a matter of jumping in. The clarity will come. If your passion is still in alignment with you, you will create magic in all the moments.

Innocence and a *Leave It to Beaver* Life

As I mentioned, we moved from East Oakland to Salem, so we could have more opportunities and less stress—and, boy, did that happen! I lived a *Leave It to Beaver* life, which was heavenly, and my parents seemed to be happy.

One of my first official, grown-up jobs at age 16 was as a waitress. It was scary and hard, but the money was needed for school clothes the following fall, and I had to help out by working in the summer.

One day, I took an order for a Coke and went into the bar to get it. When I peaked through the small window to order the drink, I saw a band setting up to play on the stage.

"Whoa!" I thought. "This is exciting! I want to *join* that band!"

I had no idea if they even needed a singer or where I was going to get the nerve to ask them. Shyness, a lack of confidence, and fear of rejection washed over me.

A song came on the jukebox: Donna Summer's "Last Dance." While I was waiting for the bartender to hand me the Coke, I started singing along with Donna, in full voice and extra loud.

One of the guys in the band stopped, looked at me, turned to another band member, and said something. He jumped off the stage and came right over to me. He asked me if I was in a band or had sung with a band before.

Of course, I said with confidence, "YES!"

I lied. Yes, I had been in the school choir and had my own little trio in school, but we weren't professional and had not played anywhere in public.

"What did I *do*?" I thought, nervously considering the possibility of being in my first professional band.

Soon after, the band called me for an audition. It was strange to ask for my parents' permission on the phone, but they gave their consent. They drove me to the audition the following week, and I was hired to be the lead singer in the band.

This was about intention, letting go, and using my voice and presence to attract my desires without knowing how. That summer, we played music in clubs and parties, and I went back to school in the fall. This was the beginning of *just going for it* in life. I was scared, but I knew what I wanted to do and acted without overthinking it and without negative self-talk. It was about the innocence and ignorance of jumping in. After you do it once, more things line up.

I was ready for the opportunity, and I showed up. No matter how afraid I was, I had courage and took the opportunity. I took the chance to look stupid and possibly be embarrassed. However, because my passion was clear with intention, *I acted.*

I was willing to not be perfect or have it all together before I engaged. Opportunities came in strange ways, but I had the initial groundwork ready. Going beyond the norm and prepping the foundation helped me be ready and gave me a small window of excitement and confidence.

My eyes were open and I made the move, even though it was scary.

Select an Accountability Partner and Discover Your Intention

Select someone who will support you as a positive accountability partner to share what you will do and are doing daily or weekly. Make sure this person has no judgment and will help you take that first step, such as a friend, coach, or person who truly cares about you and listens so you can be vulnerable.

In your journal, list the person you will call. For example:

♥   "My accountability partner will be Jennifer Parker, my best friend."

Ask yourself, "What is my desire/fire? What is my intention?"

Once you know the answers, get into action. Here are some examples of journal entries:

♥ "I need to call a few musicians I know today and see about joining their band or ask them if anyone is looking for a vocalist. If I don't know anyone, I will ask around, do the research to see who was in that field, and make my presence known in some way."

♥ "I will take my first step on Friday, August 2nd, at 2:30 PM. I will call Jennifer Parker and ask her to hear my fears before I make that call or talk to that person."

Inner Delight

You have an extraordinary story that is written or wants to be written. You have opportunities in front of you all the time. If you understand where you're going, the possibility to be brave with abandon becomes effortless.

It's time to take a chance. Jump out of and into shear fear and desire and see what happens. Practice is key. It's not necessarily simple to be who you are in every moment. Use your inner knowledge and innocent fire to ignite that movement.

Use your full self-expression to work *through you* and *for you* in ways that will surprise you … much to your inner delight!

CHAPTER 6

SAY "YES" TO YOU AND "NO" TO NEGATIVE, UNHEALTHY RELATIONSHIPS

Don't compromise yourself. You are all you've got. There is no yesterday and no tomorrow. It's all the same day.

—Janis Joplin

Stand for Your Highest Good

At some point in your life, you may experience negative and unhealthy scenarios. I had both until I finally saw that saying "yes" to myself was the direct path of alignment to my own highest good. I saw how hugely important it was to create a self-loving framework that supports and honors me first. With this positive framework, I was present and could healthily support others.

I also learned that part of aligning with myself was saying "no." However, you may experience a desire to *not* take care of yourself by checking out. You may let others walk all over you or take advantage of your kindness. You may even stand up and complain about it, but you may never do anything to shift this attitude and behavior.

Once you truly take care of yourself, you'll start to see things about yourself that you have never noticed before. If you didn't see these things on some level, you weren't paying attention. It's time to correct what needs to be corrected in your life, so you can move forward. It's time to take inventory.

Make Negotiable and Nonnegotiable Decisions

In your journal, think of negotiable and nonnegotiable things that you feel work or don't work for you.

How do you want to be treated in life? Once you know the answer, you will begin to see how the negotiable and nonnegotiable things show up, and life will begin to shift. You will feel more empowered as you quickly assess and adjust what and who you want in your life.

Nonnegotiable things include moments when you walk away because a person has crossed an important line. This behavior is usually a core way of seeing that someone else's being is out of alignment with you and they are not willing to meet you halfway.

Here are some examples:

- ♥ **Negotiable:** "I'd like everyone to put down the toilet seat when they are finished. This makes it fair for everyone using the bathroom."
- ♥ **Negotiable:** "I love it when my boyfriend brings me flowers every month as a surprise."
- ♥ **Nonnegotiable:** "Yelling and cussing hateful words in anger make me feel sick and are deeply hurtful."

- ♥ **Nonnegotiable:** "Playing gaslighting mind games is not acceptable."
- ♥ **Nonnegotiable:** "Talking only about yourself on our first date makes me feel that you are interested in impressing me and are not being present with me."
- ♥ **Nonnegotiable:** "Touching my guitar without asking is extremely rude, and I feel disrespected."

It's up to you to decide in each scenario or situation what is and is not empowering. The process creates a clear view of yourself and the people around you—in friendships, with lovers, and in your career—and acknowledges your personal boundaries. It's a guideline for your emotional well-being that will shine powerfully as healthy self-esteem and self-worth. It will be a beam of clarity, which creates a calm confidence to guide your decisive, resonant choices. This is the root system of your inner guidance, and it's time to use it!

Pay attention.

Listen and, if you're honest, you'll hear the answer.

Take Care of Yourself Right Now

When you feel out of alignment with anyone or anything, ask yourself, "How do I need to take care of myself right now?"

Take some quiet time with no distractions, so you can relax, be in the present moment, and answer the question.

By not listening to your inner voice or feelings and not acting, your problems will increase. Once you take this time, however, it becomes clear what's next and what framework you need to create for yourself, for that person, or for that situation. A daily practice of self-discovery along with quiet time will develop a muscle for hearing what you truly want and help you see a clearer path.

You will begin to see who in your life is toxic and who is draining you—even loved ones. You may be in a tangled mess and wonder why you keep answering the phone when they call. Just say "no." Stop the cycle of madness and self-victimization.

You will also see who in your life is nurturing you and feel moved to act and design a nurturing framework to live in. Your intentions and mantras will be a space and a choice for a balanced connection and a relationship.

Be patient. Ask yourself these honest questions daily until they are natural. When you see a balanced connection clearly and honestly, your desire to honor yourself will be paramount as you move into focus. You can then start to clean house on all levels.

Clarity and calm come from *choosing you first*.

Let Go

My friendship style and understanding are to listen, be present, have real interest, and share and ask questions. Then, I want all the things I give to that friendship from the other person. I had assumed that all people thought of a friendship as a give-and-take scenario, but my experiences taught me otherwise.

One particular relationship was a runaway train of painful, draining experiences and verbal abuse. Every time he and I would get together, I was always excited to connect. As I usually did, I would listen intently with an open heart and a helpful mind. If it were warranted, I would share my thoughts and ideas and hope for a back-and-forth engagement.

My excitement would be quickly overtaken by his nonstop talking, ongoing and unresolved upsets, stories of grandiosity, and ego pumping. Most of all, he had no curiosity about me and my life.

At the time, I wasn't aware of how to identify or ask for what I wanted from this friendship. I became a nonstop listening machine, always burnt out and drained. When I did offer a suggestion to solve an issue, it would usually turn into opposition, dismissal, or anger. I felt like a suppressed and uncompensated therapist. In my mind, this was not friendship or fun.

First, I regretted hanging out with him. Then I thought I would just be there for support with no comments. My next thought was, if I do that, I will need to make sure that I am willing to donate my time for our time together. I did these things for a while until, one day, I found myself avoiding his calls or making excuses not to connect. I finally woke up to the fact that I wasn't having a fulfilling relationship. I was not going down a two-way street where real friendships were nurtured, uplifted, and mutual. After a while, it became too cumbersome and unacceptable to continue.

This realization was not his issue. I needed to take responsibility for my part in the play. I needed to let go or be dragged. I realized that my experiences of feeling abused, drained, used, and unheard were mine, and I could do something about them.

I let go.

My resolution was to stop saying "yes" to things that weren't empowering to my body, mind, or spirit—just because I felt that someone needed me. I moved through my life based on what I needed to resolve my issues, and the dynamic between my friend and me was not aligned anymore.

As I cycled through things—shifting and growing—the other person was growing too, but their growth was not in my direction or in my presence. What we both agreed to—whether consciously or unconsciously—was now complete.

After I was clear about who I was, the relationship naturally began to melt away. We briefly spoke two years later, and he was still the same, but it was all good between us.

I let go with love and gratitude in my heart.

I loved me enough to say, "No, thank you."

There's no wrong or right way to decide something. There is only your choice to own your empowerment in any situation, and there is always an outcome. I can say "yes" to me and "no" to unhealthy situations and people, and then send them off with light.

Having a clear idea of who you are and what you want out of a friendship comes from your own declaration and no one else's. If it isn't a match or can't be worked out, *choose you*. If you are not choosing you, you will feel the consequences, and the outcome will most likely leave you dissatisfied.

Live By Your Own Declarations

If you feel bad, apprehensive, overwhelmed, or drained in any connection, it's time to reexamine what you want and don't want in that relationship. Figure out what is negotiable and what is nonnegotiable, and then move toward it. It's time to walk away from blind faith and attachment to something that doesn't feel good and doesn't support you to have an extraordinary life of joy.

In your journal, write your declarations, such as:

♥ "From this day forward, I am committed to saying 'yes' to me first."

♥ "From this day forward, I am committed to saying 'no' to unhealthy things and relationships. When I see or feel things in my life that are not in alignment, I will say 'no' and decide to love myself."

♥ "My declaration framework is that my friend has to show up for me, such as calling me back or texting me in a timely manner. I want to hear from them, and I want them to be curious about my life. I will not accept abuse, yelling, or condescension from my friend."

♥ "I will make sure that my friends understand what I need from our friendship. I will ask them what they need. I will not stress over things beyond my control."

Write five things your friends can do to nurture and support you. Here are some examples:

♥ "My friends can truly listen to me."

♥ "My friends can share if they are upset with something, and then we can resolve it together."

Next, write examples of negative experiences, such as:

♥ "I need to let go of my music teacher, who is amazing, but he always talks down to me. I will call him tomorrow at 10 AM to let him know how I feel."

Finally, write examples of how you feel after you take the above actions. For example:

♥ "After letting the negativity go, I feel a new sense of freedom and confidence to do the things that support my well-being. I feel empowered and calm."

The Gift of Love

Letting go is an act of love to myself and to the other person. It sends a message that I am not willing to be part of a cycle that is clearly not shifting or wanting to shift. Just because I care or love that person, staying in a situation that is unhealthy and abusive doesn't serve anyone. It is not my responsibility to try and make someone something they are not or do not want to be.

Saying "no" is just as powerful as "yes."

Letting go is a gift of love to all.

SPEAK UP AND SPEAK OUT

The most common way people give up their power is by thinking they don't have any.

—Alice Walker

Take Back Your Power

It takes courage to speak up and speak out. It also takes clarity and a willingness to start.

On a subconscious level, speaking up and out could be a way to be killed. Historically, it's an innate tail of caution, such as being shunned from a tribe and left alone in the wilderness to starve. When you speak out, you become a pariah and make waves. As a social outcast and troublemaker, you think for yourself—whether or not anyone likes what you're saying. You have the gumption to say what you think or feel, even if it is wrong or wacky in others' views.

If you want to do or say something out of the norm, you will undoubtedly feel pressure. Your throat will get dry, your pulse will quicken, and you will sweat. Then, the fear will come. You may want to run, or you can decide to shut up and take it.

♥   What do you want to say?

♥   What do you believe in?

♥   What are you passionate about but are not acting on?

COURAGE

Be honest with yourself and ignore the fearful internal conversations that have been stopping you. Answering these questions gives you insight and a clear foundation of confidence. Be willing to do what it takes and share your beliefs with others. Remember: No one knows what you think, feel, want, or believe in until you share it.

Be prepared for feelings of discomfort when you speak. You will need to develop this muscle, and it will get stronger. Even though it may feel judgmental, others are probably worried and focused on their own fears and their own ideals and not what you are going to say or how you'll say it.

Speaking up and out is about stepping up and getting behind your truth and full self-expression. You are leaning into the *risk-taking* side of yourself, which is key. The sooner you contribute, the less time you have to generate self-doubt and hold yourself back from expressing yourself freely. Jump in! It gets easier as you practice being vulnerable and transparent with yourself and others about who you are. Bravery comes at a price, but you will experience your inner riches.

Share your inner feelings, thoughts, and desires with others. Sometime things are just not worth saying, but sometimes they are—even when it can be challenging. Follow your intuition. When it counts, dive in, share, and hold your ground. That type of confidence is truly infectious.

There may be times where the topic is too hot—either for you or for someone else. In these cases, you may choose not to share or reveal things. It is your intuitive call, and it is not fearful. However, in situations where you don't want to talk about something for fear of ramifications and possible serious upsets, and you're afraid that it will lead to disappointments or possible disapproval, this is not self-expression. It is fear. The difference is that one is done from care and respect, and the other is a reaction of survival and self-suppression.

There may also be times when it's best to make your voice be heard in a way that expresses you and gets your point across without major confrontations. This situation can be tricky but possible.

Be attuned to each situation and decide whether or not it is appropriate to share. Remember: Others' opinions of you are none of your business. This mindset will keep you away from a fear-conscious trap.

Vote with Your Pocketbook

If you are talking about picketing outside of a certain place or telling someone that you are angry, both situations can be challenging. You may not want to go to jail just to picket for your feelings or beliefs. You have to weigh the consequences for each and possibly choose other options. Follow your heart and intuition and choose the best power options for speaking out.

Here are some examples of my power options:

- ♥ I make my opinion or voice heard by voting with my pocketbook.
- ♥ I write letters that make my voice heard.
- ♥ I join organizations that support effectively what I want to see shifted.

As another example, if you are a person who has a problem with Amazon and Jeff Bezos's company policies, you can do several things:

- ♥ Start a campaign with signatures to have your ideas and voice heard.
- ♥ Stop shopping at Amazon.
- ♥ Stop shopping at Whole Foods Market.
- ♥ If you are an employee, speak your voice by walking off the job, talking to the press, and petitioning a lawsuit against them.

Be creative. There are always options if you look deeper with clear intent and are willing to take the consequences.

I have stopped using a lot of products that impact my beliefs. I look for alternatives that are healthier and have less impact on the planet. I feel empowered, freer, and more self-expressed for speaking out and choosing alternatives that align with me. It's effective, and I uplift and inspire others around me.

Empower Yourself with Action

In your journal, write at least two things that you are afraid of saying to someone. Then pick one of these things, set a date to share it with the person you were thinking about, and add it to your calendar to complete it. Here's an example of what you could write:

♥ "On Tuesday the 2nd at 10:30 AM, I will call Pete Farmer. He continues to be late for all our meetings, and I am feeling disrespect for him."

Next, list some businesses that are not in alignment with what you believe and think about how you can make a difference. For example:

♥ "Walmart is not environmentally green because they use plastic bags. I will write to their head company about alternatives, and I will stop shopping there."

Doing *something* helps you feel in action and empowered around things that you are passionate and moved to speak up about. This will leave you with well-practiced and long-term courage in your life.

If you commit to something and end up not doing anything, that's fine. Don't beat yourself up! Just recommit and try again. Keep trying until you build up courage to say something and do something. You'll feel much freer.

Write Down Your Triumphs

What are you inspired to say and do? In your journal, write down the heading, "My Triumphs," and break them down in daily, weekly, monthly, and yearly sections.

There is one important rule: This is about YOU sharing YOUR experience. It is not a truth. The intention is not to make someone or something wrong when sharing. Think a bit deeper and find a balanced way to share and express your insights.

Understand your position of responsibility in the matter. This understanding will give you a clearer mind, a more centered space, and a more empowered place to stand in and share. The intention is to be complete and freed up on some level.

Listening and Inner Guidance

Where in your life can you make an impact, feel fully expressed, make a difference, and be freed up to be you? You have a unique expression and purpose. It's up to you to remember yours and decide how you want to share it.

If you're thinking from a place of pure self-expression, your inner knowledge will guide you to the things, people, and places you need at any given moment. Add love and compassion for others and look from a higher place.

Ask questions and be curious as to why this is happening to you or to the situation, and then listen for the answer or just ask. This process is not easy, and you can forget and react to so many things.

Ask yourself, "What am I afraid of? Why am I afraid of it?"

Wait for a minute and listen. You will soon hear the answer, and you'll be on a path of celebrating you and your freedom.

ASK FOR WHAT YOU TRULY WANT AND EXPECT THE MAGIC

Magic is a state of mind and being
if you just let it happen.

—Glenda Benevides

Asking Is Giving and Balance Is Freeing

Sometimes knowing what you truly want is a cloudy mess, let alone knowing who to ask to support you. It could be as simple as asking a friend to help you sort out your garage, leaving you more time to focus on your TED talk audition in three days, which you've been avoiding.

It sounds simple yet, for most of us, asking is hard. You may not want to inconvenience anyone and would rather suffer, subconsciously sabotaging and setting yourself up for stress and drama—even failure. You may have even been taught this way of thinking through family or cultural beliefs.

Actually, the mental exercise of coming up with reasons not to ask for help is a lie that keeps you from connections and support. By asking, you give another person an opportunity to grow and show up too. If you have completed all the steps in this book so far, you'll have a clearer idea of what you may need to ask for.

The concept of speaking up and speaking out in Chapter 7 is related to asking for what you want or need. Teaching each other how you need to be treated and feeling free to ask and give are huge steps.

Ask yourself these questions:

♥ "Am I willing to be honest and ask someone to support me in my time of need?"

♥ "Am I willing to reach out and ask instead of suffering alone?"

If you stop for a minute and ask yourself these questions, you will have your answers. Action in the face of your fear is courage.

When you ask for help, you'll see who's truly there for you and provide them with the opportunity to give to you. This is a huge gift to others, but they may not know how to help or how to be demonstrative enough to ask if you need help.

For those who are not paying attention, your request for help gives them an opportunity to serve and be served in return. This act of serving each other brings gems of the heart. When you turn away from other people's assistance, it doesn't give them a chance to feel good, share, or be uplifted. When asking for support—even when it feels weird—do it anyway.

You may have been taught not to ask for anything, and you may suffer in silence to avoid being impolite and lowly. Doing things for others is honorable and leads to goodness. If each person allows the other to give, both are uplifted.

Asking is giving and balance is freeing.

In the Flow and Letting Go

I was getting ready to take my annual trip to London to see my best friend. I thought it would be nice to pick out something special in advance to do while I was there and not just wing it this time. Of course, winging it is fun and usually flowing inside the parameters that I love and am familiar with, such as history (especially medieval) and swords.

While searching online, I found some information about the Key Ceremony at the Tower of London. They were now allowing commoners to experience the ceremony that locks the tower at night. This was something special, unique, and definitely linked to history!

As I read on, the website said that you had to handwrite and mail a letter to them and, once they received this letter, they would let you know when you could come through. This process was not trip-friendly and could take months. Bummer! I was leaving in two weeks. Feeling disappointed and with a heavy heart, I let it go.

In London, I shared my story of excitement and then serious disappointment with my best friend while we were waiting in the London Underground (the Tube).

She immediately said, " Oh, yeah? You're going!"

"Did you hear what I said?" I asked her. "This is an official advance request and a requirement in order to go on a night tour inside the Tower of London. You know … locking of the Tower gates. It's called the Key Ceremony."

My friend looked at me and again said, "You're going!"

I thought she was crazy and didn't want to explain again that it was an official access process. I let that go too!

A week later, I said, "Hey, I'm off to the Tower. Want to go?"

She agreed, and we were off.

We spent most of the day walking through the levels of the White Tower and the dungeon, seeing the crown jewels, eating yummy scones with clotted cream, watching the handsome tower guards parading in formation at set times, and hanging in my favorite room: St. Thomas's Tower, which is a bedroom built between 1275 and 1279 by Henry III's son Edward I, above Traitors' Gate.

While we were in Edward's bedroom, we decided to take a short rest. We casually and naturally sat down in the stone cubby window seat in his bedroom. I laughed to myself that this was not an official area to sit in, but we did it as if it were our own room. In our little private nook, we talked and relaxed while peering out the window at the River Thames and Tower Bridge, laughing and commenting on life in the 1400s. It was so magical, like a scene out of a romance movie! The whole day was like that—tea and scones with clotted cream and wonderfully handsome men in medieval costumes. We felt transported.

Back in the White Tower at around 5 PM, as we stared at Henry VIII's armor, one of the yeoman warders yelled to all the tourists, "Closing time!"

We headed down the spiral stone steps toward the back-courtyard exit. Just as we were about to walk out, my best friend saw a very tall and handsome guard in full uniform. He had a princely way about him—magnetizing and mesmerizing.

As she and I looked at each other, I said, "Go! Get a picture with him!"

We were both stunned.

I said again, "Do you want to a get picture with him? Go!"

We moved toward him and he asked, "Who are you?" and then minutes later, "What are you ladies doing later on tonight?"

We both told him that we had no plans.

With a calm demeanor, he said, "Well, how would you both like to join me tonight for the Key Ceremony?"

I thought, "*What?* No way!"

In my moment of amazement, shock, and meltdown, my eyes opened wide, my mouth dropped, and I swiftly said, "Yes!"

I felt 13 years old again, going on my very first date with the boy I was secretly and madly in love with. Actually, I wasn't in love with the guard, and it wasn't my first date, but it was an invitation to an impossible thing out of nowhere. It was like magic, like a god granting my wish. It was a strange and exciting chance of a lifetime.

From this experience, I learned that all things are possible, even when you can't see it or know the end result. I had shared my desire, my excitement, and my disappointment.

I was in the flow and letting go.

I let it be.

I stayed open.

I was in action.

Asking for what you truly want and expecting it to happen— no matter what you may think—is a key factor in creating a magically aligned and expressed life.

Take Time to Breathe

In your journal, write down what you truly want and how you will ask for support. For example:

- ♥ **"I truly want to be listened to.** The next time I am sharing my heart with my partner, I am going to ask them to listen with an open mind and heart."

- ♥ **"I want to go to the new symphony next week.** A good friend has tickets, but I can't afford them right now. I'm going to ask her if she will let me go with her as a trade. I'll ask her tonight on our weekly call."

♥   **"I want help cleaning my back guest bedroom.
     I have company coming in two days.** I usually do
     everything by myself, and I never ask for help as I don't
     want to inconvenience anyone. I really need some
     support this time for moving the big furniture. I will
     ask my son to come over and help me for an hour."

See it happen, know that it's happening, and then let go and
expect it!

Stay with your desire, focus on your feelings and visions of
joyous manifestation, and then let go. You will know if you are
in alignment with what you're wanting by how you honestly feel
deep down and if your flow is present. Meaning, signs, and doors
open effortlessly with a synchronistic style, and you choose them.

Action plays a final part in choice around what you are
moved to say or do. This is how things move from wishing to
tangible life experiences. Many delightful surprises show up that
you never knew you wanted when you are aligned in your choice
of action.

BE BY YOURSELF AND TAKE THE TIME TO REGENERATE

Demonstrate love by giving it
unconditionally to yourself.

—Glenda Benevides

Your Personal Pledge to You

It's not easy to shut out the world, the job, the kids, the duties, and other things in your life. You may not take or make time for yourself. Although the reasons for doing this are legitimate, your needs may often come last or not at all.

If this is the case in your life, you are in for a huge breakdown, and it's only a matter of time—*guaranteed*. That breakdown can come in many forms, such as divorce, chronic anger, sadness, depression, or illness. I've seen it time and time again with myself and with others who have become sick or felt helpless and powerless to shift their behavior. This cycle is not self-love and does not support you in any way.

As you develop the new flows and processes in this book, you will be able to spot the areas that need to shift. You can finally sit back and honestly put in place some time *for you*. You will begin to see YOU coming back, and your inner voice will be present.

Taking care of you first—even if it's one day a week or a half hour—to be quiet, to rest, and to let your mind wander and wonder. It's easier said than done, and you will have to choose between commitment and self-love. When you choose you first, you will see the invigorating benefits of rejuvenation.

Taking care of yourself is to be *self-full* in life. Some people think that self-care is *selfish*. It's not. This manipulating lie has been perpetuated for hundreds of years—keeping people in line; working long hours; feeling oppressed, guilty, and worn down; and eventually getting sick.

Airlines always tell adults to put on their masks before their children. As you practice putting on your mask first, you will see your life improving exponentially. You'll immediately feel better and experience more excitement, more patience, and more clarity in knowing your needs and desires. You'll have more energy naturally to do all the things you want to do.

Shutting out the world and telling others "no" or being by yourself to quiet your mind can be scary. Distractions rush in to help you avoid hidden or buried truths. Eventually, the truth always arises, and it is up to you to embrace it with fortitude. It's time to choose YOU and all that goes with it. Isn't this what being honest and alive are all about?

Do one thing a week that gives you time to yourself and freedom with no distractions. Look at perceived commitments—the things that only you can take care of—and challenge them. Are you really the only one who can do these things?

Ask yourself, "Am I the one truly choosing this commitment? Did I want to?"

Commitments to loved ones should never leave you drained, tired, and unable to fulfill your own life. It might take time to think outside the box and arrange your life into one that serves you as well. For example, maybe you have to pay someone to pick up your children at school, so you can go for a run or take a class.

Ask yourself, "How can I have it all?"

People are stronger than you think. They can rise to many challenging occasions without your constant presence and help. Sometimes things can wait. Decide whether you want to say "yes" or "no."

Start with 15 minutes of personal time. Move up to 30 minutes and then a few hours once a week. Eventually, this personal time will take on a new meaning and significance for you. It should look like this every day.

It is your personal pledge *to you*.

Nothing Changed
Until I Changed It

In addition to my regular job, there were always additional schedules to support others when they needed it. I ran errands, took calls, and worried about things that ultimately didn't affect me. I never realized that I could run my own life and not be a victim of it.

Now, nothing has changed and everything has changed. I still do things for people and my business, but I start my day with a routine that makes me feel healthy in my body and spirit and is aligned with me. My self-imposed "me" time consists of a short meditation, deep-breathing exercises, and stretching. Two times a week, I exercise and practice yoga.

This routine nurtures me and gives me a foundation of peace, clarity, energy, and love to share. It supports me to have a strong sense of myself and well-being. I am ready to be on top of my world in my day and in my life, and I am more centered and peaceful. It gives me time to regenerate, think, ponder, and just wander around if I want to. Everyday "me" time is in the flow with the structure of the day. If I forget to take this time for myself, I feel it right away. I feel off and sometimes even upset. When I love myself, it feels great, and I feel free.

If I find myself jumping into things without checking in first, I am living unconsciously and am not in touch with my emotional and physical health and well-being. I will have accidents and be angry, frustrated, overwhelmed, victimized, rude, thrown, and pushed. This detrimental outcome can lead to resentment, bad feelings, and other crazy roller-coaster moments.

I try to be mindful by not scheduling things into my quiet time. I consciously create schedules that fit into my life and not around others' lives. Sometimes it's a little more work, but it is worth it in the long run. With time and practice, it has become much easier.

Setting Up "Me" Time

Look at your daily and weekly schedules at the beginning of each week. Sunday night might be best to see what the weekly duties and outside demands look like. Note what you have to do and whom you have to do it for. Decide which activities are negotiable and which are nonnegotiable.

Ask yourself, "Where can I add some time for me?"

Add personal time in your calendar and set your phone alarm for it, which will keep you on track. You may experience resistance, but just *do it*. It'll work if you say "yes" and surrender. Do not use your brain to keep track of your times and schedules. If you do, you are setting yourself up to fail because you have practiced forgetting yourself for so long. This behavior is hard to shift, so use tools to help yourself. Eventually and naturally, you will add "me" time and schedule things occasionally. Make it fun and something you look forward to.

After the one-day-a-week practice, move up to scheduling "me" time every day in your calendar. It is very important to add this time to your calendar to make sure that you don't forget YOU. If you stick to this plan, you will reap the benefits of feeling free, at ease, and in the flow, while still making sure things are accomplished.

In your journal, record your plan for setting up "me" time:

♥ "I will schedule time for myself to do whatever I want—relaxation and fun every Saturday with no interruptions or to-dos for others. This day is set aside for me."

♥ "I will take 15 minutes (from 9 to 9:15 AM) every day. During these 15 minutes, I will visualize my intentions for the day."

♥ "On Mondays, I'll take an hour to do my yoga, take a walk, read, or have coffee with a friend."

Living a Goddess Lifestyle

After shifting your habits to honor and love yourself authentically—no matter how small the changes are—you will see a difference in your attitude and in others around you and feel less stress. You'll see the value of taking 15 minutes a day in your health and desire to be more fulfilled. This will lead to powerful self-expression and support your courage in your day-to-day life.

This shift is the beginning of a badass goddess lifestyle, and others will treat you accordingly and see you in a new light. Your choices will be made from what serves all concerned—especially you! You will experience an immediate ability to decide "yes" or "no" in each situation.

Be wise with your time and your energy. It's all you have. When it's gone, it's gone.

CHAPTER 10

CHOOSE A COMMUNITY THAT YOU LOVE AND THAT SUPPORTS YOU

Owning your story and loving yourself
through that process is one of the
bravest things you'll ever do.

—Glenda Benevides

CHOOSE A COMMUNITY THAT YOU LOVE AND THAT SUPPORTS YOU

The Los Angeles School
of Hard Knocks

When I was living in northern California, I decided to move to Los Angeles to shift my career into something that was more in step with my age. This was the beginning of my first mistake.

The year before this decision, I recorded my second album with a dear friend who was in the film industry. He told me that if I came to Los Angeles, he would mix the album. He also said that he had good friend living there who was an amazing singer and was successful on Broadway in *Rent* and *Aida*.

My friend set up a meeting with this singer/actor as he loved my newest song, "Wait for Love," which he said would be a perfect project to work with him. I was very excited and inspired by that offer!

When we met, we had a special chemistry. He was a seasoned professional and a fabulous vocalist too. I was entranced, enchanted, and smitten.

About a year or so later, my subconscious mantra of "I'm not good enough" led me to rethink my career path and ongoing questions of how I could stay in my industry and be relevant. My inner belief was that I was now too old and therefore couldn't be successful. This is a common story for many people in the music industry. I realized that this story was "old thinking" and a lie, and I wasn't going to let it run my life.

I had a new idea: Blend music and stories together, like a musical. Even though I didn't like musicals, I thought I would make it different.

I shared my story idea with the Broadway singer/actor to see if he wanted to partner on this idea. I felt that my idea and this artist would lock me into a chance at longevity in music along with a paycheck. He loved the idea and told me that he would love to partner with me. I was very honored and excited that someone of his stature would want to work with me. It was on!

Unfortunately, I didn't create clear agreements with him. I just jumped into a partnership like a novice: no structure, no rules to play by, and no power for me. I had the money, the connections, and a good idea; he saw an easy mark and took control with confidence. I don't believe he did anything with malice, but he was a good hustler, and survival was his game.

I told myself that he knew better than I did and that we were good friends. I gave up my power and voice. I was also the one giving him money whenever he needed it and rides to wherever he wanted to go.

He redesigned my show without my input, and I said nothing. I was supposed to have the lead part, and he ended up making all the decisions and writing all the music. I allowed myself to be pushed into the positions of producer and executive producer. I thought I was investing in my future career; he thought I was investing in his. He was the king, and I was one of his female servants. This on-the-mat training was painful. I attended the Los Angeles School of Hard Knocks.

I spent the next two years living in Los Angeles where I spent $10,000 of my small inheritance from my dad's passing and another $1,600 a month in a one-room apartment, playing the starving artist. I paid all the bills, did all the leg work, and collected all the negative heat from people he promised money to without telling me—all with a team of two.

Even with the intensity, drama, and crazy-making antics, my show launched with a full house! I did it all *and* stayed in the black. I learned how to put agreements in place with love, support, and integrity, and nurture myself and others. While I was licking my wounds, I saw my part in the design of my life and the choices I made where I didn't speak up. My self-esteem was tragic, but I could shift it.

After that huge mindset shift, I started to listen more deeply, share my truth, and act on things no matter what. I let people know who I was and where my boundaries were. I was willing to be my own friend with love and support.

This was the second time that I had done this to myself based on my beliefs that were running my choices. The hurt and disappointment cut deeply, and I had to shift them. I stepped forward and did not let anyone run over me. I spoke my truth to others and did not let people take advantage of my goodness and generous nature—especially when my intuition said "no" and "I'll pass."

My next step was to go home, create a new self-declaration, and get some goddess support conversations going!

My Deluded Mantra

Once I was home, I asked myself several questions and put the answers in my declaration of independence. After much soul-searching and deep reflection, I began to talk to my closest friends who would be honest with me. I felt lost, like a failure on the edge of depression, and I seriously needed help.

I asked them, "Who am I for you? How do you see me?"

They each gave me a reality check and told me that I *wasn't* a failure. They saw me as someone who never gave up on people and situations in life. Stunned and blown away in that moment, I saw the greatness in who I was in my community.

I realized that the story I was telling myself—the unconscious-conscious mantra—was a delusion and a lie. This story made me feel small, giving away my power to others whom I thought knew better than I did. I thought they had the answers.

I was not choosing situations or people in a clear and powerful way because I wasn't clear. I was waiting for someone else to tell me the answers. I was choosing and thinking from underlying feelings of:

- ♥ "I'm not good enough."
- ♥ "Others know better."
- ♥ "Others are the authority on things, and I'm not."
- ♥ "I'm selfish if I ask for what I want."

I wasn't showing up as the brightest part of myself. These stories keep me from having what I wanted in life in an empowered way. Actually, it was just the opposite: It bordered on victim mentality.

I saw the pattern and how it was costing me huge amounts of time and money for hardly any benefit, and then shifted my "I'm not good enough" mantra. This mantra was keeping me from freedom, love, full self-expression, and ultimately joy. I realized that I was letting the community I was attracting and surrounded by take advantage of my kindness. They knew I would give them the things they were asking for without too many questions on my part.

After these realizations, I learned, healed, forgave, and eventually let go. Once I was willing to put my loving attention on my balance, honesty, and clarity, I gained huge confidence. I learned to step into having it all.

The truth was—and is—that *I am good enough.*

Write Your Declaration of Independence for YOU

Take a minute to look into any areas in which you want to shift, and then set your new path with a declaration of independence for YOU. The community you generate from this decision will be one of respect, honor, honesty, care, support, and love. It's very insightful and empowering!

In your journal, you may write:

♥ "When meeting someone new, I will keep an open heart and an honest, watchful eye."

♥ "I will share my truth, no matter what."

♥ "I will create powerful expectations for friendships."

♥ "In any new business relationship, I will walk away from situations that are not in alignment with me and that do not feel good or serve my highest good."

♥ "I will only have relationships that are healthy partnerships with love, respect, and care."

See Your Part in the Scenario

How you behave is a direct reflection of your conscious and unconscious beliefs and patterns. Once you have some mastery at being quiet and hearing your inner thoughts, you'll start to see who you are being and whether or not it works, and then see the connection of how it directly relates to how you are acting or reacting. It will also be self-evident that you are not achieving what you're truly desiring in life.

Wherever you go, there you are. You cannot escape you! If you are consistently having issues, complaints, and the wrong people in your life, the only thing that is the same is "you."

If you hear yourself complaining about who is in your life and all the unfair things and people making your life hell, take a moment and see your place in the equation. Who are you being? Is your behavior giving you what you want?

Complaining indicates that what you are doing and who is in your life are not in alignment with you. This analysis can answer a lot of questions as to why you're upset, not satisfied, pissed off, unhappy, unsettled, and angry. Question why you are always chasing something or have no time to listen because you're always waiting to talk. Maybe you're being a know-it-all. Maybe you're jealous or frustrated. If you're feeling any of these things, it's time to take a look in the mirror and see your part in the scenario.

Once you've figured it out, you can perhaps get some coaching to help shift your mindset or have a straightforward conversation with someone about what you are feeling or what your experience is with them.

Most of all, it might be time to let go, walk away, and call it complete. Take an honest look and decide who in your life goes, who stays, and how you are going to adjust your attitude in relationship to others. Deep down, are you committed to a life that works for you? That you are taking responsibility for? That you are ready to share and be accountable for? Can you let go and forgive everything, with no strings attached?

Are you ready to say, "no more," and move on, with insights and knowledge of what you want and who you want in it?

CHAPTER 11

CHOICE = GROWTH = UNSTOPPABLE LIFE

Never give up, for that is just the place
and time that the tide will turn.

—Harriet Beecher Stowe

Reality, Dreams, and Perseverance

In the winter of 2004 in the south of France, my musical colleague/good friend and I attended a music conference called MIDEM (International Music Market) in Cannes. I was so excited to possibly meet up with record companies and producers. This opportunity would give me the option to sell my music directly to a record company that would license my music or even sign me to their label.

This was also the first time in the world of music that artists had do-it-yourself options. It was an exciting new era in the music business—a dawn of an open digital market for all to play in. This was never the case from the 1950s to the early 2000s. You had to be signed by a major label if you wanted a large audience and to make a living. It was a secret society that was breaking down, and most independents were beginning to feel empowered.

I was a music veteran with a possibility of selling my music and enhancing the next level of my career. I had been writing original music seriously for the previous seven years, and this was an opportunity of a lifetime—or though it seemed.

The MIDEM marketplace was alive. More than 20,000 people gathered from around the world, open for new blood and new business, and I was going to get my chance by my own volition.

Prior to 2000, it seemed that only the lucky few were signed to a major label, but there was a cost. It was not about luck, magic, or talent; it was a willingness to sell your soul if you had the chance. You also had to have an insatiable desire—a willingness to do anything and everything. You were expected to move in the right circles, have something sellable, and most likely be under the age of 20.

Control + manipulation + greed = slavery. Prince had it right when he wrote "Slave" on his face. There was no free expression, which equals the death of an artist (hence the 27 Club with members Jim Morrison, Janis Joplin, and Jimi Hendrix).

All I ever wanted was to have a music label help me get my music into the world on a larger level and then be able to make a living from that music. It wasn't the "fame" factor; it was the "make a difference" factor. Ever since I was 13 years old, my life was in music, and I was going to make my living doing that.

I was ready! I was hitting the next level. I was driving my dream and my business. I was working toward my destiny: to share my talent and gifts with the world. Well, I *thought* I was. My innocence and ignorance didn't serve me, but my inner stability and intuition did.

Standing at the top of the Palais des Festivals et des Congrès stairs in Cannes at 9 AM was the most surprising, rectifying, and unfortunate moment of my life. This was a five-day conference, and it was the day after I had picked up my badge. As I stood in line with thousands of artists and worldwide companies, the reality that I was not alone started to sink in.

At the top of the 30-foot descent into the palace, I was so freaked out and overwhelmed that I couldn't move. All I could do was watch the hordes of artists, streaming in all around me. I was lost in a sea of competition, and all my fears were intensely present. Darkness began to overcome my mind and run down my whole body.

Suddenly, I heard a shrieking voice in my head: "Who am *I* to be here? Oh, my God! I am not good enough. Turn around and leave *now* … NOW! You're too old for this." Depression blanketed my whole body and my mind chanted, "My career was over 20 years ago! Leave now. It's over. *Go home.*"

I felt as if I had just lost the battle in a 100-year war, and I was given notice that I had 24 hours to live.

With deep sadness and held-back tears, I quickly left and ran to my apartment. The feelings were unbearable, as if my whole life were over and every dream that I had was null and void. My purpose for living was executed on those palace stairs.

I opened the apartment door, repeating to myself, "I'm not good enough. What a fool! My time was over 20 years ago. Why am I here?"

My friend came around the corner and asked, "What's wrong?"

"I am feeling like a fool," I told him. "My career was over 20 years ago, and I don't even know it! This revelation started at the top of the stairs at the palace. I am sick to my stomach!"

He looked me in the eye and said, "Your story is not true. Your time is *now*. It is a new day filled with new possibilities!"

He was a self-made man who had spent his life overcoming many obstacles. He lived in Alabama and Michigan and dealt with many forms of racism. My shocking moment of illusion and self-pity seemed so small, which stopped me from giving up. In that moment, I remembered that there are much larger challenges for people than my life's illusions.

I moved my mental lies out of the way. His presence in my life made me find my core, and that compassion gave me the sense I needed. I went to the palace the next day and networked my ass off! I was back and not alone.

Give Up Your Stories

A poor man can rise to his success, and a rich man can live in the street. It's better to embrace your poor man and rise! Ride out the waves of your lies because they too shall pass.

In your journal, describe a few situations where you said any of the following statements:

- ♥ "I give up."
- ♥ "I quit."
- ♥ "I'm not enough."
- ♥ "I'm not lovable"

See what story, conversation, or statement had you saying and believing that you couldn't do something you wanted to do.

You can face things that frighten you. Go beyond your fear and commit to doing them, even if you hear your negative self-talk. Get back in the game, get on the mat, and give it another shot. You will learn new things about yourself, your perseverance, and what it takes to have courage—all of which will lead you into confidence and full self-expression.

Don't think … act!

CHAPTER 12

LET GO AND BE COMPLETE

When I let go of what I am,
I become what I might be.

—Lao Tzu

Illusions and Inner Truth

When you do things that you feel are best for your heart, sanity, health, and overall well-being, you pause ... sometimes for too long. You go down the road with a loud, annoying inner voice that wants you to feel obligated, guilty, wrong, and just bad.

You stop yourself from doing or saying all the things you would love to do or say in order to shift and release the pressures you feel. This behavior continues the pattern and doesn't work in the long term. You feel more out of alignment with who you are than ever before. The life drains out of your spirit, and your chaos remains.

If you stepped back and looked, you would see that feelings of obligation and guilt are illusions. You've brought forward these old stories from past scenarios and beliefs or from a time that you believed them. Unfortunately, this behavior unconsciously keeps you "in check and enslaved," attracting the wrong things, the wrong people, and unsuccessful ways of dealing with them.

When you do not shift or let go, you feel uncomfortable and emotionally upset. Signs of sickness appear, and constant confusion is present. For example, pressure and stress may be signs that something is off.

By Myself, For Myself, and Inside Myself

Some of the hardest relationship moments I've had were when I unconditionally kept a relationship going—to the detriment of my own soul—when a certain friend (I'll call him Mr. Crazy) would reach out to me. When I started to feel the pain drain, I didn't want to answer the phone or conveniently had no time to do anything with this person when I would answer it. I felt bad and guilty about my behavior because I loved this person.

It was no way to have a friendship—full of angst and fear of answering the phone and then eventually not wanting to run into him on the street for fear of being bombarded with negativity. Finally, it was resolved, but I had to hit bottom to hear my inner voice and recognize my boundaries.

Another friend and I went out to dinner. Mr. Crazy was there, and the three of us ended up eating together. As we sat in the beautiful restaurant, Mr. Crazy filled the room with the aggressive sound of his voice: combative, nonstop, not listening, and righteous. There was no back-and-forth conversation, just ego running out of his mouth. I felt sorry for my other friend because he was chill and tried to answer Mr. Crazy's testosterone-filled questions.

In a quiet moment, my calm friend answered one of the questions. Mr. Crazy—feverishly smoking a vape inside the restaurant—raised his voice and displayed a bombastic attitude toward my friend, which was strange as the attack had nothing to do with the question that was asked.

We left. It was a strange and weird experience over nothing. I was disgusted, shocked, and afraid.

On the way home, I told myself, "That's enough!"

I wasn't available for any time with this person. I was disengaged. He knew that what he did was unwarranted and rude, and there was no need to call it out. It would take time to let go, and I was on the road to full completion.

Time passed, and we both ceased talking to each other. There was no confrontation. It was as simple as letting go and being complete with something or someone without them needing to be there or agree. It sometimes comes by yourself, for yourself, and inside yourself. It doesn't always have to be done directly with the person because that may not be possible.

I am still on a friendly note with this person. I still dearly care for him, but I do not need to be a close friend or hang out in serious connected ways anymore. We are not aligned, and it is okay. I am grateful for the time and experience we shared, and I am sure that he is on his own journey.

Rework Your Little Voice

It's time to let go of the situation or the people in your life that are not in alignment with who you are today. It's time to rework your little voice.

Letting go of relationships and telling the people involved your inner truth is not for the faint of heart. Sometimes it's very complicated and you probably don't want to hurt anyone, let alone be in some conflict around the issues at hand. This experience is confrontational, and courage is required.

You may say, "If I am a good friend, I will hang in there and be there for them."

If you have said this to yourself with your relationships, at what cost? If you are not being you and can't freely speak your truth, are they seriously a good friend? Are you a good friend for lying about how you feel or what you want?

When a mutual energy resonance is not there or is not returned, you may ask yourself these questions:

♥ "Is this worth what I am putting into the relationship?"

- ♥ "Am I emotionally drained and unfulfilled when I see this person?"
- ♥ "Do I feel taken advantage of emotionally?"
- ♥ "Am I avoiding the phone when they call?"
- ♥ "Do I take a long time to call them back?"

If you answer "yes" to any or all of these questions, it is a sign that it's time to pay attention and act.

You may try to communicate in loving ways with the intention of having a healthy, balanced connection. Then, when it isn't successful, you feel tortured. When this happens, look at your addiction to suffering—the kind that makes you a complaining martyr.

For example, when the phone rings and it's them, your face grimaces and you get stressed, but you pick up the phone anyway. Why did you pick it up when you knew that they would talk your ear off, never change their story, keep complaining about the same situations, and never want to find a solution? They're not the least bit curious about you or your life and almost never ask. If they do ask, the conversation goes right back to them and their drama, and you feel abused again. You keep coming back to try to help or to be their friend because you assume that they'll turn it around. This behavior is the definition of insanity: doing the same thing over and over and expecting a different result.

In these situations, it's up to you to make the choice to let go. If you are seeking alignment, then letting them go is an evolutionary step. Sometimes things have just run their course, and what you need to learn and serve is not out of loyalty or alignment with them. If it's not a healthy interaction or a two-way street, stop being the punching bag of your inner spirit. It's time to let go and be complete with all that has happened. Forgive and move on.

When you tell yourself that you love them and want to be there to help them—even though you are suffering—ask yourself, "Is that love?"

The highest quality gifts in a friendship are to be present, supportive, healthy, and a true listener. You may try to create a mutual agreement on how to be with each other, but it may not yield the best possible result. Sometimes you can side with them or show them other ways of looking at things by sharing.

This sharing approach does not make them wrong or have them see *your* truth. It's about giving them the space to hear themselves and then choose if your insights might work for them too with no attachment. This behavior has the qualities of being open, loving, kind, caring, and loyal.

Take a look at the people in your life and select those whom you feel have been the best you can be with. Ask yourself:

♥ "Have I been clear in my communication, or is it just not working?"

- ♥ "Am I fully self-expressed?"
- ♥ "Does the sharing come from both sides?"
- ♥ "Do both parties listen to each other and want to participate?"
- ♥ "Are sentiment, fear, judgment, and guilt the only things keeping us together?"

Make a list (or it may be only one name) of the relationships that do not work for you anymore. Let them go with love. If you do write down names, burn the list and send it off with love and forgiveness for you and them. If you don't need this burning ritual, just be grateful, consciously choose to let go in your way, and be complete.

Do not allow yourself to be held hostage by YOU. Don't let your inner monologue of illusions keep you tied into something you honestly don't want. Choose a healthy way of being and living. If you cannot do it on your own, talk to someone who gets you, and then let go.

Make a plan and stick with it—no matter what—and see how you feel after a week.

Choose Love and Harmony

The trial is with you—not other people. There may be conflicts, but you can look at them, resolve them, and then shift your thoughts to attain balance and well-being. No one else can make it right for you. You have to choose it. This choice doesn't make the other person right or wrong. In reality, that issue is none of your business.

The only business you have is *you*. You design how you handle life situations, and the keys are about how you react and interact. At the end of the day, wherever you go, there you are!

Are you doing your life's work in harmony? Are you thriving?

Some things you just have to let go and be complete for you. The rest will work itself out.

CHAPTER 13

THE GODDESS IS TO LOVE

Sister, mother, friend, healer, lover—
the bravery to be unapologetic is
what makes you the goddess.

—Glenda Benevides

You Are the Goddess of Your Realm

The high priestess is the goddess with the leadership and creative qualities of the magician. The number "11" is spiritually sensitive, charismatic, cooperative, and independent. This is the power of love and balance.

Be brave enough to be unapologetic for who you are. At the end of the day, that's all there is, and it is serious self-love. Loving yourself in a genuine way leaves a space to love others with the highest intentions. Being in appreciation and sincere acknowledgement for what you're creating each day leaves a wake of healthy relationships around you.

Design your life the way you truly want it. There is no time to waste your amazing life force and gifts on things that aren't serving you emotionally, mentally, physically, or spiritually. It doesn't serve anyone!

You've seen an upset waitress or a guy at your local food store who can't be bothered to look up at or even talk to you with joy in their voice and heart. This negative interaction is like an infection that's been passed on. When it comes to you, it sets off your day by making everyone feel uncomfortable, sad, or frustrated and never furthers satisfaction or joy. For some people, it is their only interaction with anyone, and they are left with negativity.

Can you see how your call to love in action is so imperative?

Negativity spreads and has a direct effect. It's never an isolated situation, so don't be fooled. Your joy or anger gets on everyone, whether or not you think it does. It's a vibration that goes out to the universe and eventually comes back in some form. Then you wonder why life is not working. This negative vibration can be avoided if you take the time to know *you*.

Try to understand what you are truly passionate about and what drives you to wake up every day and say, "Thank you! I love my life, and I am so grateful to be fully who I am and who I am becoming!"

This gratitude is the most important thing for a life that's worth living with balance and health showing up in magnificent ways.

It is profound to have courage to face the everyday things you love and fear and still be in action. Once you adopt a daily mantra of action with courage, you will find your energy soar to places that are surprising, unusually spectacular, and often noteworthy.

It often takes trial and error to find out who you are now and what you desire now. The key is to get on the road and discover it. It's an ongoing journey. Try it out, fail, and then try something new. See what sticks as you move forward. Moreover, take the time to ask yourself thoughtful, mindful questions and look for your answers.

Play with new ideas, even if you have no agreement from anyone. Be bold! Remember: They are not YOU, and they are not living YOUR life. Part of this equation is to keep people in your life who honor and accept you—for you—and let the others go.

Most of all, make *you* your business.

Be brave enough to sit with your fear conversations in your head and address them. Ask yourself these questions:

- ♥ "What am I afraid of?"
- ♥ "Are my fears real?"
- ♥ "Am I starving?"
- ♥ "Am I homeless?"

Often, fears are stories to keep yourself safe or keep you from being right. This safety zone may keep you frozen and unable to take any steps. "Frozen" is not where you thrive—except, of course, if you encounter poisonous snakes! Keep looking for your truth.

Fear of rejection is a big consideration when it comes to life's passions. Being RIGHT and avoiding emotional wounds keep you from having what you've always wanted and dreamed about. Even if someone says "no" at some point, it means that you have to keep going and align with the right people.

No one can tell you or keep you from anything. If you believe that they do have this power over you, it will keep you in a victim mode, and you will always be fighting against a perceived external enemy, which is an illusion. You design your future and your freedom.

Take your insights, information, and passion and choose a direction. Take the time and take the step. Do something that furthers your path of a dream fulfilled. Make that move. What are you waiting for?

Take that first step, no matter what. Create a community that supports you and wants to align and play with you in your vision. It's simple and yet you have to work for it. There are no shortcuts to waking up, choosing you, and embracing that ever-evolving new YOU. You have to focus and work for it.

This is the juicy part of any journey. This is where you learn, grow, and live into your dreams. Allow yourself to shed others' fears and the old delusions of who you think you are—the delusions you bought hook, line, and sinker.

It can be done—step by step, day by day, and minute by minute. You can have it if you design it and jump in. This is the journey to full self-expression. Embrace your passion and courage and design your reality.

Love is an everlasting gift you can give to yourself and to others if you have courage to be yourself fully and expressed.

Be present that you are the choice maker, the truth seeker, the gratitude believer, and the visionary doer—the goddess of your realm. Rest in the knowledge that it's all coming from *within* you *to* you. You just have to give it the green light and keep your eye on the road and on your destination.

You are here to learn, share,
express and live in joy …
you have the courage!

20 RULES TO LIVE BY

COURAGE

1. Practice embracing who you are fully and breathe in deeply. Do breathing exercises a few minutes each day.

2. Make time each day to be present to life around you. Get outside and see the magic happen. Be still, look, and listen with your whole being.

3. For the first thing every morning, close your eyes and spend a few moments being grateful for what you have and love every day.

4. Take an account of what is positive in your daily life and write it down in your journal.

5. Be willing to find your true passion—something you have always wanted to do—and step toward it, even if it's a small pleasure.

6. Change happens whether or not you think it does, so embrace it.

7. Be straight with yourself. Look at what's not working and what is, and then create from there.

8. See your default settings and design new ones.

9. Be willing to identify old beliefs that are not working and practice releasing them.

10. Create new habits that are aligned with who you say you are. Practice one habit at a time.

11. If someone is not in alignment with who you are, if you are in turmoil, and if you are suffering in some way, let go and move on.

12. Refuse to participate in drama-trauma games of any kind. Change the subject with a smile.

13. What others think is none of your business.

14. Success in life is a mindset and a choice. You say how it goes.

15. No matter what you think you are creating, know that your life is a precious moment. Play!

16. Your choices create your reality.

17. Honor your word as if your life depended on it. It may.

18. Relationships with others are precious, so treat them as such. You may learn something.

19. Show up for yourself, and then give that gift to others.

20. "No" is NO, "yes" is YES, and "maybe" is NO.

Made in the USA
Middletown, DE
11 July 2022

68932955R00086